"Rich Thoughts, Rich Life: Transforming Your Mind for Abundant Wealth"

"True wealth lies not in material abundance, but in the richness of one's mind – where creativity, wisdom, and resilience flourish, transcending any external measure of fortune"

BISHAL CHANDRA SHIL

Rich Thoughts, Rich Life: Transforming Your Mind for Abundant Wealth

TABLE OF CONTENTS

INTRODUCTION: THE MINDSET OF WEALTH

PART I: UNDERSTANDING THE POWER OF YOUR MIND

Chapter 1: The Psychology of Prosperity

Chapter 2: Getting to know Your Brain: Wiring it for Wealth

Chapter 3: Overcoming Your Limiting Beliefs

PART II: CULTIVATING A WEALTHY MINDSET

Chapter 4: Mastering self-discipline and delayed gratification

Chapter 5: Abundance Consciousness

Chapter 6: Practicing Gratitude and visualization

PART III: YOUR BLUEPRINT FOR FINANCIAL SUCCESS

Chapter 7: Setting Clear Goals and Intentions for Your Life

Chapter 8: Multiple Streams of Income

Chapter 9: Investing for Long-Term Growth

PART IV: NAVIGATING CHALLENGES AND OVERCOMING OBSTACLES

Chapter 10: Understanding Fear and The Value of Failure

Chapter 11: Imposter Syndrome

Chapter 12: Building Resilience and Persistence

PART V: MINDFULNESS TOOLS FOR YOUR EVERYDAY WEALTH BUILDING

Chapter 13: Mindful Spending and Budgeting

Chapter 14: Developing Healthy Money Habits for a Lifetime

Chapter 15: Balancing Work, Wealth, and Well-being

CONCLUSION: EMBRACING YOUR JOURNEY TO FINANCIAL FREEDOM

APPENDIX: RESOURCES FOR FURTHER GROWTH AND DEVELOPMENT

Introduction: The Mindset of Wealth

In a world brimming with opportunities and possibilities, the pursuit of wealth is often viewed through a narrow lens of material acquisition. Yet, beneath the surface lies a profound truth: true wealth begins in the mind. Welcome to "Rich Thoughts, Rich Life: Transforming Your Mind for Abundant Wealth", a transformative journey that transcends conventional notions of prosperity and delves deep into the realms of consciousness, psychology, and self-mastery.

In these pages, we embark on a quest to unlock the secrets of the wealthiest individuals not merely in terms of their bank accounts but in the richness of their mindset. For it is here, in the fertile landscape of our thoughts and beliefs, that the seeds of abundance are sown. The journey to financial freedom is not solely paved with strategies and tactics; it is paved with the bricks of mindset, resilience, and unwavering determination.

As you embark on this odyssey, prepare to challenge the very fabric of your beliefs about wealth and success. Gone are the days of viewing prosperity as an elusive dream reserved for the fortunate few. In this book, we embrace the radical notion that wealth is not a destination but a journey — a journey guided by the compass of our minds.

Part I sets the stage by exploring the fundamental principles underlying the power of the mind in shaping our financial reality. From understanding the psychology of prosperity to rewiring our brains for abundance, we lay the groundwork for a paradigm shift that will revolutionize your approach to wealth creation.

In Part II, we delve into the art of cultivating a wealthy mindset — an inner landscape adorned with the fertile soil of self-discipline, abundance consciousness, and gratitude. Here, you will discover the transformative power of aligning your thoughts and beliefs with the boundless potential of the universe, opening the floodgates to a life of unparalleled abundance.

Armed with a newfound sense of clarity and purpose, Part III equips you with actionable strategies for navigating the labyrinth of financial success. From setting clear goals and diversifying your income streams to making prudent investment decisions, you will learn to harness the power of your mind to manifest your wildest dreams into reality.

Yet, no journey to wealth is without its challenges. In Part IV, we confront the fears, doubts, and setbacks that threaten to derail our progress. Through resilience, perseverance, and an unwavering commitment to growth, you will emerge from the crucible of adversity stronger, wiser, and more determined than ever before.

Finally, Part V invites you to integrate mindfulness into every facet of your wealth-building journey. From mindful spending and budgeting to cultivating healthy habits and striking a harmonious balance between work and well-being, you will learn to infuse every moment of your life with intention, purpose, and presence.

As you embark on this transformative odyssey, remember this: the journey to becoming a mindful millionaire is not a sprint but a marathon—a marathon of self-discovery, growth, and infinite possibility. So, arm yourself with courage, curiosity, and an insatiable thirst for knowledge, for the path to wealth is not for the faint of heart. But rest assured, dear reader, the rewards that await you are beyond your wildest imagination.

Part I: Understanding the Power of Your Mind

In the opening segment of "Rich Thoughts, Rich Life: Transforming Your Mind for Abundant Wealth," we embark on a profound exploration into the foundational principles that underscore the influence of our minds on our financial destinies. Here, we delve deep into the realms of psychology, neuroscience, and human behaviour to uncover the hidden forces at play in shaping our perceptions, decisions, and ultimately, our financial outcomes.

Chapter 1: The Psychology of Prosperity

In the first chapter, we embark on a journey into the fascinating realm of the psychology of prosperity. We explore how our subconscious beliefs, ingrained from childhood and shaped by societal norms, can either propel us toward wealth or hold us back in a cycle of scarcity. Drawing upon real-life examples from individuals who have transcended their upbringing and societal conditioning to achieve extraordinary success, we unravel the intricate web of thoughts, emotions, and beliefs that govern our relationship with money.

For instance, consider the story of Oprah Winfrey, who rose from poverty and adversity to become one of the most influential and affluent figures in the world. Despite facing numerous challenges and setbacks early in life, Oprah's unwavering belief in her own potential and her refusal to be defined by her circumstances propelled her to unparalleled heights of success. Her story serves as a powerful reminder of the transformative power of mind-set in overcoming adversity and creating a life of abundance.

Through thought-provoking insights and practical exercises, readers are encouraged to examine their own beliefs and attitudes toward wealth, challenging ingrained notions of scarcity and limitation to embrace a mindset of abundance and possibility.

Chapter 2: Rewiring Your Brain for Wealth

Building upon the foundation laid in the first chapter, we delve deeper into the fascinating field of neuroscience to understand how our brains can be rewired for wealth. Drawing upon cutting-edge research and real-life case studies, we explore the concept of neuroplasticity — the brain's remarkable ability to reorganize and rewire itself in response to new experiences and stimuli.

We examine how habitual thought patterns and behaviours shape the neural pathways in our brains, influencing our perceptions, decisions, and ultimately, our financial outcomes. Through the lens of neuroplasticity, we learn that our brains are not fixed entities but dynamic and adaptable systems capable of profound transformation.

For example, consider the case of Tony Robbins, renowned motivational speaker, and author, who has dedicated his life to helping people transform their lives through the power of mind-set. Through his ground-breaking work, Robbins has demonstrated how individuals can rewire their brains for success by replacing limiting beliefs and negative thought patterns with empowering beliefs and positive affirmations.

By understanding the principles of neuroplasticity and harnessing the power of our brains to create new habits and behaviours, readers are empowered to break free from the chains of scarcity and limitation, forging a path toward financial abundance and fulfilment.

Chapter 3: Overcoming Limiting Beliefs

In the final chapter of Part I, we confront head-on the formidable barrier that stands between many individuals and their financial aspirations: limiting beliefs. These deeply ingrained beliefs, often rooted in fear, self-doubt, and past failures, can sabotage our efforts to create wealth and success.

Through insightful anecdotes and practical strategies, we explore how to identify and overcome these limiting beliefs, replacing them with empowering beliefs that align with our highest aspirations. Drawing upon the experiences of real-life individuals who have transcended their own limiting beliefs to achieve remarkable success, we uncover the transformative power of mind-set in shaping our financial destinies.

For instance, consider the story of Sara Blakely, founder of Spanx, who revolutionized the fashion industry with her innovative line of shapewear. Despite facing numerous rejections and setbacks in her journey to success, Blakely remained steadfast in her belief in herself and her vision, refusing to let fear or self-doubt stand in her way. Her story serves as a powerful testament to the importance of cultivating a mind-set of resilience, optimism, and unwavering self-belief in the face of adversity.

Part II: Cultivating a Wealthy Mind-Set

"Cultivating a Wealthy Mind-set" embodies the art of fostering a mind-set that is conducive to prosperity and abundance, both financially and personally. It involves nurturing beliefs, attitudes, and habits that align with the principles of wealth creation and fulfilment. This subtle transformation begins within, where individuals gently awaken to the innate potential within themselves to manifest abundance and success.

In this journey, individuals delicately cultivate a rich inner landscape, sowing the seeds of positivity, resilience, and gratitude. They recognize the power of their thoughts and intentions, nurturing them with care and attention to create fertile ground for prosperity to flourish. Through subtle shifts in perspective and perception, they begin to see opportunities where others see obstacles, blessings where others see challenges.

Cultivating a wealthy mind-set involves a subtle dance between ambition and contentment, as individuals strive for greatness while remaining grounded in the present moment. It is about embracing the journey as much as the destination, finding joy in the pursuit of growth and self-discovery. With each gentle step forward, individuals cultivate a deeper sense of abundance and fulfilment, enriching not only their lives but also the lives of those around them.

Ultimately, cultivating a wealthy mind-set is a subtle yet profound process of transformation—a journey of awakening to the boundless potential within oneself and the world. It is about embodying the essence of abundance, prosperity, and well-being in every aspect of life, embracing the subtle whispers of intuition and inspiration that guide us towards our highest potential.

Chapter 4: Mastering Self-Discipline and Delayed Gratification

In the journey towards financial success, mastering self-discipline and delayed gratification are indispensable qualities. Self-discipline involves the ability to control one's impulses, emotions, and actions in pursuit of long-term goals. Delayed gratification is the practice of sacrificing short-term pleasures for greater rewards in the future. Let's explore these concepts in detail.

Consider the example of two individuals, Alex and Sarah, both aspiring entrepreneurs. Alex lacks self-discipline and often gives in to immediate desires, such as spending money on luxury items or indulging in leisure activities instead of working on his business. As a result, he struggles to make progress towards his goals and faces financial difficulties.

On the other hand, Sarah understands the importance of self-discipline and delayed gratification. She sets specific financial goals and creates a budget to manage her expenses effectively. Despite the temptation to spend impulsively, Sarah exercises restraint and prioritizes investing in her business and personal development. Over time, her disciplined approach pays off, and she achieves significant success in her ventures.

By mastering self-discipline and delayed gratification, individuals like Sarah can stay focused on their long-term objectives, resist impulsive spending habits, and make wise financial decisions that lead to wealth accumulation.

Chapter 5: Abundance Consciousness

Abundance consciousness is a mind-set that acknowledges the limitless opportunities and resources available in the world. It involves shifting from a scarcity mentality, which focuses on limitations and lack, to an abundance mind-set that embraces prosperity and abundance in all areas of life.

Imagine two people, Mark and Emily, who have different perspectives on abundance. Mark operates from a scarcity mind-set, constantly worrying about not having enough money or opportunities. As a result, he tends to hoard resources, avoid taking risks, and feels envious of others' success.

In contrast, Emily embodies abundance consciousness. She believes in the abundance of opportunities and approaches life with optimism and gratitude. Instead of dwelling on what she lacks, Emily focuses on her strengths, seeks opportunities for growth, and celebrates the success of others. As a result, she attracts positive experiences, meaningful connections, and financial abundance into her life.

Practicing abundance consciousness involves affirming abundance through positive affirmations, visualization, and acts of generosity. By adopting this mind-set, individuals can unlock their full potential, attract abundance into their lives, and cultivate a sense of fulfilment and gratitude.

Chapter 6: Practicing Gratitude and Visualization

Gratitude and visualization are powerful tools for cultivating a wealthy mind-set and manifesting financial abundance. Gratitude involves acknowledging and appreciating the blessings and abundance already present in one's life. Visualization, on the other hand, entails vividly imagining and experiencing future success and prosperity.

Let's consider the example of Rachel, who incorporates gratitude and visualization into her daily routine. Each morning, Rachel starts her day by expressing gratitude for the blessings in her life, such as her health, relationships, and opportunities. By focusing on what she already has, Rachel cultivates a positive mind-set and attracts more blessings into her life.

Furthermore, Rachel practices visualization to manifest her financial goals and aspirations. She creates a vision board adorned with images and affirmations representing her desired outcomes, such as financial abundance, business success, and a luxurious lifestyle. Through regular visualization exercises, Rachel aligns her thoughts, emotions, and actions with her goals, thus increasing the likelihood of achieving them.

By practicing gratitude and visualization, individuals like Rachel can reprogram their subconscious minds, overcome limiting beliefs, and attract wealth and abundance into their lives. These practices serve as powerful tools for transforming dreams into reality and creating a life of prosperity and fulfillment.

Part III: Your Blueprint for Financial Success

"Blueprint for Financial Success" is like having a clear roadmap to reach your money goals. It's a simple plan that helps you manage your money wisely and achieve the things you want in life. Just like a blueprint helps builders construct a building step by step, this blueprint guides you in building your wealth over time.

Imagine it as a set of instructions or guidelines that show you how to make smart choices with your money. It includes things like setting goals for what you want to achieve financially, creating a budget to track your spending and saving, and finding ways to grow your money through investing.

With this blueprint, you'll have a clear picture of where you're headed financially and the steps you need to take to get there. It's like having a compass that keeps you on track towards your financial dreams.

So, whether you want to buy a house, start a business, or retire comfortably, having a blueprint for financial success can help you turn your dreams into reality in an easy and manageable way.

Chapter 7: Setting Clear Goals and Intentions for Your Life

Setting clear goals and intentions is the cornerstone of achieving financial success. Without a clear direction, individuals may find themselves drifting aimlessly, lacking focus, and failing to make meaningful progress towards their financial aspirations. In this chapter, we delve into the importance of setting clear goals and intentions and provide practical strategies for defining and pursuing them.

Consider the example of John, a recent college graduate who dreams of becoming financially independent. Despite his ambition, John finds himself unsure of where to start and what steps to take to achieve his goals. However, upon reflecting on his aspirations and values, John decides to set clear, specific, and achievable financial goals.

John's goals include paying off his student loans within five years, saving a certain percentage of his income each month towards an emergency fund and investments, and eventually starting his own business. By articulating his goals and intentions, John gains clarity and purpose, which fuels his motivation and determination to take action towards realizing his dreams.

Throughout his journey, John regularly revisits and adjusts his goals based on his evolving priorities and circumstances. By staying committed to his vision and taking consistent action, John makes significant strides towards financial success and ultimately achieves his goals.

Chapter 8: Multiple Streams of Income

In today's dynamic and unpredictable economy, relying solely on a single source of income may not provide the financial security and stability individuals desire. Creating multiple streams of income is essential for diversifying risk, maximizing earning potential, and achieving financial independence. In this chapter, we explore the concept of multiple streams of income and share strategies for generating passive and active sources of revenue.

Take the example of Sarah, a working professional with a passion for photography. In addition to her full-time job, Sarah leverages her photography skills to create multiple streams of income. She offers photography services for weddings, events, and portraits on weekends, sells prints and digital downloads of her work online, and teaches photography workshops and courses.

By diversifying her income streams, Sarah not only increases her earning potential but also hedges against economic downturns and job insecurity. Moreover, Sarah enjoys the flexibility and autonomy that come with managing her own business ventures, allowing her to pursue her passion while generating additional income streams.

Through strategic planning, resourcefulness, and perseverance, individuals like Sarah can build a portfolio of diverse income streams that support their financial goals and aspirations, providing financial resilience and freedom.

Chapter 9: Investing for Long-Term Growth

Investing is a fundamental strategy for building wealth and achieving long-term financial growth. However, navigating the complex world of investments requires knowledge, diligence, and careful planning. In this chapter, we explore the principles of prudent investing and share strategies for building a diversified investment portfolio geared towards long-term growth and wealth accumulation.

Consider the example of Michael, a young professional with a keen interest in investing. Recognizing the power of compounding returns and the importance of building wealth over time, Michael adopts a disciplined approach to investing. He conducts thorough research, seeks guidance from financial advisors, and diversifies his investment portfolio across various asset classes, including stocks, bonds, real estate, and mutual funds.

Moreover, Michael prioritizes long-term growth over short-term gains, focusing on investments with strong fundamentals and growth potential. He regularly monitors his portfolio, rebalances asset allocations, and stays informed about market trends and economic indicators.

Over time, Michael's prudent investment strategy pays off, as his portfolio steadily grows in value, outpacing inflation and providing financial security for the future. By investing for long-term growth, individuals like Michael can build wealth, achieve financial independence, and realize their dreams of a secure and prosperous future.

In conclusion, setting clear goals, diversifying income streams, and investing for long-term growth are essential components of a blueprint for financial success. Through diligent planning, disciplined execution, and perseverance, individuals can chart a course towards financial freedom and abundance, realizing their aspirations and creating a legacy of prosperity for generations to come.

Part IV: Navigating Challenges and Overcoming Obstacles

Navigating challenges and overcoming obstacles in finance is a bit like steering a ship through stormy waters. Along the way, you might encounter rough seas in the form of unexpected expenses, market downturns, or personal setbacks. But with the right strategies and mind-set, you can navigate through these challenges and come out stronger on the other side.

Think of it as having a toolkit filled with resources to help you weather any financial storm. This toolkit might include things like an emergency fund to cover unexpected expenses, a diversified investment portfolio to cushion against market volatility, and insurance policies to protect against unforeseen risks.

When faced with financial challenges, it's important to stay calm and focused. Take stock of your situation, assess your options, and develop a plan of action to address the issue at hand. Whether it's tightening your budget, seeking additional sources of income, or adjusting your investment strategy, there are always steps you can take to overcome obstacles and keep moving forward.

Remember, setbacks are a natural part of the financial journey, but they don't have to derail your progress. By staying resilient, adaptable, and proactive, you can navigate through challenges and emerge stronger and more confident in your financial future.

Chapter 10: Understanding Fear and the Value of Failure

Fear and failure are inevitable parts of the journey towards financial success. However, understanding their dynamics and learning from them can be transformative experiences that propel individuals towards greater resilience and growth. In this chapter, we explore the nature of fear, the value of failure, and strategies for overcoming them.

Consider the example of Maria, an aspiring entrepreneur who dreams of launching her own business. Despite her passion and determination, Maria grapples with fear of failure and uncertainty about the future. However, instead of letting fear paralyze her, Maria chooses to confront it head-on by reframing her mind-set.

Maria understands that failure is not a reflection of her worth or abilities but rather an opportunity for growth and learning. With this perspective, she embraces failure as a natural part of the entrepreneurial journey and approaches challenges with resilience and determination.

Moreover, Maria recognizes that failure can provide valuable insights and lessons that ultimately contribute to her success. By analysing her mistakes, seeking feedback, and adapting her approach, Maria transforms setbacks into stepping stones towards her goals.

Through her journey, Maria discovers that facing her fears and embracing failure not only strengthens her resilience but also expands her capacity for innovation and creativity. Ultimately, Maria's willingness to confront fear and embrace failure propels her towards greater success and fulfilment in her entrepreneurial endeavours.

Chapter 11: Imposter Syndrome

Imposter syndrome is a psychological phenomenon characterized by feelings of self-doubt, inadequacy, and the fear of being exposed as a fraud despite evidence of one's accomplishments and competence. Many individuals, including those on the path to financial success, grapple with imposter syndrome and its debilitating effects on their confidence and performance.

Take the example of David, a talented financial analyst who excels in his career but struggles with persistent feelings of self-doubt and insecurity. Despite receiving accolades and recognition for his work, David constantly worries that he doesn't deserve his success and fears being exposed as an imposter.

As David navigates his journey towards financial success, he realizes that imposter syndrome is a common experience shared by many high achievers. Instead of succumbing to self-doubt, David seeks support from mentors, peers, and mental health professionals to address his negative self-talk and develop strategies for overcoming imposter syndrome.

Through introspection and self-awareness, David learns to challenge his negative beliefs, celebrate his achievements, and cultivate a sense of self-worth independent of external validation. By reframing his mind-set and embracing his unique strengths and abilities, David breaks free from the grip of imposter syndrome and unleashes his full potential for success.

Chapter 12: Building Resilience and Persistence

Resilience and persistence are essential qualities for navigating challenges and overcoming obstacles on the path to financial success. In this chapter, we explore the importance of resilience and persistence and share strategies for developing these critical skills.

Consider the example of Sarah, a budding entrepreneur who faces numerous setbacks and obstacles in her business ventures. Despite encountering failures and disappointments along the way, Sarah refuses to give up on her dreams. Instead, she embraces resilience and persistence as guiding principles that fuel her determination and perseverance.

Sarah understands that success rarely comes without setbacks and failures. She views obstacles as opportunities for growth and learning, rather than insurmountable barriers. By cultivating resilience, Sarah bounces back from setbacks with renewed determination and creativity, finding alternative solutions and approaches to achieve her goals.

Moreover, Sarah recognizes the power of persistence in achieving long-term success.

She maintains a steadfast focus on her vision, consistently taking action towards her goals despite challenges and setbacks. Through her unwavering commitment and determination, Sarah overcomes obstacles, achieves her aspirations, and builds a legacy of resilience and perseverance.

In conclusion, understanding fear, overcoming imposter syndrome, and cultivating resilience and persistence are essential for navigating challenges and overcoming obstacles on the path to financial success. Through introspection, support, and perseverance, individuals can unlock their full potential, achieve their goals, and create a life of abundance and fulfilment.

Part V: Mindfulness Tools for Your Everyday Wealth Building

Imagine having a toolbox filled with simple but powerful tools to help you build wealth every day. That's what mindfulness tools for everyday wealth building are like. These tools are easy-to-use techniques that can help you make smarter decisions about money and stay focused on your financial goals.

One of the main tools in this toolbox is mindful spending and budgeting. This means paying attention to where your money is going and making intentional choices about how you use it. By tracking your expenses and setting a budget, you can make sure you're spending in line with your priorities and saving for the things that matter most to you.

Another tool is developing healthy money habits. This could include things like automating your savings, avoiding impulse purchases, and regularly reviewing your financial goals. By making these habits a part of your daily routine, you can gradually build wealth over time without feeling overwhelmed or deprived.

Finally, balancing work, wealth, and well-being is an important mindfulness tool for everyday wealth building. This means finding a healthy balance between your career, your finances, and your overall happiness and well-being. By prioritizing self-care, setting boundaries, and staying connected to your values, you can create a more sustainable and fulfilling approach to building wealth.

Overall, mindfulness tools for everyday wealth building are all about bringing awareness and intentionality to your financial choices. By incorporating these tools into your daily life, you can create a solid foundation for long-term financial success and security.

Chapter 13: Mindful Spending and Budgeting

Mindful spending and budgeting are essential practices for cultivating financial discipline, achieving financial goals, and building long-term wealth. In this chapter, we explore the principles of mindful spending and budgeting and provide practical strategies for incorporating them into everyday life.

Consider the example of Emily, a young professional who struggles with impulse spending and overspending on unnecessary purchases. Realizing the importance of mindful spending, Emily adopts a proactive approach to managing her finances. She creates a detailed budget that outlines her income, expenses, and savings goals, allowing her to track her spending habits and identify areas for improvement.

Moreover, Emily practices mindfulness when making purchasing decisions, taking the time to evaluate whether a purchase aligns with her values and priorities. By adopting a mindful approach to spending, Emily avoids impulsive purchases and focuses her resources on what truly matters to her, such as experiences, personal development, and financial security.

Through consistent practice and self-awareness, Emily transforms her relationship with money, cultivating a sense of empowerment and control over her financial decisions. By embracing mindful spending and budgeting, individuals like Emily can make informed choices that support their financial goals and aspirations, leading to greater financial freedom and well-being.

Chapter 14: Developing Healthy Money Habits for a Lifetime

Developing healthy money habits is essential for achieving financial stability and prosperity over the long term. In this chapter, we explore the importance of cultivating positive money habits and share practical strategies for developing and maintaining them throughout life.

Take the example of James, a middle-aged professional who realizes the need to improve his financial habits to secure his future and provide for his family. James commits to developing healthy money habits, such as saving regularly, living below his means, and investing wisely for the future.

James prioritizes financial education and seeks guidance from financial advisors to make informed decisions about budgeting, saving, and investing. He sets specific financial goals and creates a plan to achieve them, breaking down larger objectives into manageable steps.

Moreover, James cultivates habits of consistency and discipline, automating his savings and investment contributions to ensure he stays on track towards his goals. By integrating healthy money habits into his daily routine, James lays the foundation for long-term financial success and security for himself and his loved ones.

Through dedication, perseverance, and self-discipline, individuals like James can develop healthy money habits that serve them well throughout life, enabling them to achieve their financial goals and live a life of abundance and fulfilment.

Chapter 15: Balancing Work, Wealth, and Well-being

Achieving balance between work, wealth, and well-being is essential for holistic success and fulfilment. In this chapter, we explore strategies for maintaining a harmonious balance between career aspirations, financial goals, and personal well-being.

Consider the example of Sarah, a successful entrepreneur who finds herself consumed by work and neglecting her physical and mental health. Recognizing the importance of balance, Sarah prioritizes self-care and well-being as integral components of her overall success and happiness.

Sarah establishes boundaries between work and personal life, carving out time for relaxation, exercise, and social connections. She also prioritizes activities that nourish her mind, body, and soul, such as meditation, yoga, and spending time in nature.

Moreover, Sarah takes a proactive approach to managing her finances, setting aside time each week to review her financial goals, track her progress, and adjust her strategies as needed. By maintaining a healthy balance between work, wealth, and well-being, Sarah achieves greater fulfilment and satisfaction in all areas of her life.

Through mindful spending and budgeting, developing healthy money habits, and balancing work, wealth, and well-being, individuals can cultivate a life of abundance, prosperity, and well-being. By integrating mindfulness tools into their everyday lives, they can create a solid foundation for long-term financial success and fulfilment.

Conclusion: Embracing Your Journey to Financial Freedom

As we reach the conclusion of this book, it's essential to reflect on the transformative journey you've embarked upon towards financial freedom. Throughout the chapters, we've explored the multifaceted aspects of cultivating a wealthy mind-set, navigating challenges, and implementing practical strategies for building long-term wealth and prosperity. Now, as you stand at the threshold of your financial journey, it's time to embrace the lessons learned and take empowered steps towards a future of abundance and fulfilment.

Your journey to financial freedom is not merely about accumulating wealth or achieving material success; it's a profound exploration of self-discovery, growth, and empowerment. Along the way, you've confronted fears, overcome obstacles, and embraced failure as stepping stones towards your goals. You've discovered the power of resilience, persistence, and mindful living in shaping your financial destiny.

Embracing your journey to financial freedom means honouring your unique path and trusting in your ability to create the life you desire. It's about aligning your actions with your values, aspirations, and vision for the future. Whether you're pursuing entrepreneurship, investing in your career, or charting a new path towards financial independence, remember that every step you take is a testament to your courage, determination, and resilience.

As you move forward, keep in mind the importance of setting clear goals, cultivating healthy money habits, and maintaining a balance between work, wealth, and well-being. Embrace mindfulness as a guiding principle in your financial decisions, approaching each choice with intention, awareness, and integrity. Remember that wealth is not solely measured by the size of your bank account but by the richness of your experiences, relationships, and contributions to the world.

Along your journey, you may encounter setbacks, challenges, and moments of doubt. Embrace these experiences as opportunities for growth and learning, knowing that every obstacle you overcome brings you closer to your goals. Surround yourself with a supportive community of mentors, peers, and loved ones who uplift and inspire you to reach new heights.

Ultimately, achieving financial freedom is not the end goal but rather a means to live a life of purpose, fulfilment, and impact. Embrace your journey with gratitude, courage, and enthusiasm, knowing that you possess the power to create the life of your dreams. As you step into the limitless possibilities of your future, remember that the greatest wealth lies within you — your resilience, creativity, and unwavering commitment to living a life of abundance and joy.

Embrace your journey to financial freedom with open arms, knowing that each step you take brings you closer to the life you envision. Your path may twist and turn, but with clarity of purpose and steadfast determination, you will navigate towards a future filled with prosperity, fulfilment, and freedom. May your journey be blessed with abundance, and may you continue to inspire others with your courage, wisdom, and generosity along the way.

Appendix: Resources for Further Growth and Development

Congratulations on completing your journey towards financial freedom! As you continue to pursue personal and professional growth, this appendix provides a curated list of resources to support you on your path. Whether you're seeking to deepen your understanding of financial principles, enhance your personal development, or explore new opportunities for growth, these resources offer valuable insights, tools, and guidance to help you thrive.

1. **Financial Education Resources:**

   - Books: Explore a selection of books on personal finance, investing, and wealth-building to expand your financial knowledge and skills. Recommended titles include "Rich Dad Poor Dad" by Robert Kiyosaki, "The Millionaire Next Door" by Thomas J. Stanley and William

D. Danko, and "The Intelligent Investor" by Benjamin Graham.

- Online Courses: Enroll in online courses and educational programs offered by reputable institutions and experts in the field of finance. Platforms like Coursera, Udemy, and Khan Academy offer a wide range of courses on topics such as budgeting, investing, retirement planning, and financial literacy.

- Podcasts: Listen to podcasts hosted by financial experts and industry professionals for valuable insights, tips, and advice on managing your finances and building wealth. Popular podcasts include "The Dave Ramsey Show," "The Tim Ferriss Show," and "The Tony Robbins Podcast."

2. Personal Development Resources:

- Self-Help Books: Discover books on personal development, mind-set, and success principles to empower yourself and unlock your full potential. Recommended reads include "Atomic Habits" by James Clear, "The Power of Now" by Eckhart Tolle, and "Mindset: The New Psychology of Success" by Carol S. Dweck.

- Meditation and Mindfulness Apps: Incorporate mindfulness practices into your daily routine with meditation apps like Headspace, Calm, and Insight Timer. These apps offer guided meditations, breathing exercises, and mindfulness techniques to reduce stress, enhance focus, and cultivate inner peace.

- Personal Growth Events: Attend seminars, workshops, and conferences focused on personal development and self-improvement to connect with like-minded individuals and gain valuable insights from thought leaders in the field. Look for events hosted by organizations such as Tony Robbins' Unleash the Power Within and Brendon Burchard's High Performance Academy.

3. **Entrepreneurship and Business Resources:**

- Business Books: Explore books on entrepreneurship, leadership, and business strategy to sharpen your entrepreneurial skills and mindset. Recommended titles include "The Lean Startup" by Eric Ries, "Start with Why" by Simon Sinek, and "Good to Great" by Jim Collins.

- Online Business Communities: Join online communities and forums for entrepreneurs and business professionals to network, share insights, and collaborate with peers. Platforms like LinkedIn Groups, Reddit's Entrepreneur subreddit, and Facebook Groups offer valuable resources and support for aspiring and seasoned entrepreneurs alike.

- Business Coaching and Mentorship: Seek guidance from experienced entrepreneurs and business mentors who can provide personalized advice, support, and accountability on your entrepreneurial journey. Consider joining mentorship programs, mastermind groups, or hiring a business coach to accelerate your growth and success.

4. Financial Planning and Advisory Services:

- Financial Advisors: Consult with certified financial planners (CFPs) and investment advisors to develop personalized financial plans tailored to your goals, risk tolerance, and time horizon. Look for advisors with reputable credentials and a fiduciary duty to act in your best interests.

- Wealth Management Firms: Consider partnering with wealth management firms and private banking services for comprehensive wealth management solutions, including investment management, retirement planning, estate planning, and tax optimization strategies.

- Robo-Advisors: Explore automated investment platforms and robo-advisors that offer algorithm-based portfolio management and investment recommendations at a lower cost than traditional advisory services. Popular robo-advisor platforms include Betterment, Wealthfront, and Vanguard Personal Advisor Services.

5. Additional Resources:

- Financial Websites and Blogs: Explore reputable financial websites and blogs for up-to-date news, analysis, and insights on the economy, markets, and personal finance topics. Recommended resources include Investopedia, The Motley Fool, and NerdWallet.

- Financial Software and Tools: Utilize financial software and tools to manage your money, track your expenses, and monitor your investments. Popular tools include Mint for budgeting and expense tracking, Personal Capital for investment tracking and retirement planning, and TurboTax for tax preparation.

As you explore these resources and continue your journey towards growth and development, remember that learning is a lifelong pursuit. Stay curious, remain open to new opportunities, and never hesitate to invest in yourself and your future. May these resources serve as valuable companions on your path to success and fulfilment in all areas of your life.

THE
END